The Paper Chain of Kindness

Tracey Roegiers

Illustrated by Jeanine Henning

Halo
PUBLISHING
INTERNATIONAL

Halo PUBLISHING INTERNATIONAL

Halo Publishing International
7550 W IH-10 #800, PMB 2069,
San Antonio, TX 78229

First Edition, May 2025
ISBN: 978-1-63765-791-1
Library of Congress Control Number: 2025909472

Halo Publishing International is a self-publishing company that publishes adult fiction and non-fiction, children's literature, self-help, spiritual, and faith-based books. Do you have a book idea you would like us to consider publishing? Please visit www.halopublishing.com for more information.

To my family, for your endless
love and belief in me.

To my friends, for your wholehearted
encouragement and support.

To my students, for your kindness,
which inspires me.

This book is for you. Thank you for being
such a special part of the chain!

Lara gave Joe a big hug!

Jen said thank you to Tony 5 times today.

Jack helped Regina to pick up her supplies.

Tommy let a friend go ahead of him in a line

Rose held J hand

se she scared.

helped Jack feel welcome.

Regina zipped up Nicole's coat!

Nicole invited Kristin to join her group.

Tony shared his veggies with Jen.

One sunny morning, Tommy and the other students listened as Ms. Tracey gathered them on the carpet to hear something special.

"This year we are starting a new project," Ms. Tracey said, smiling. "It is called the Kindness Chain. Every time a student is caught being kind, by a teacher or another student, they will get to choose a paper link of their favorite color. Their name and the act of kindness will be written on the link, and we will display it on the classroom wall. When the chain stretches from one corner of the classroom to the other, we will have a small celebration. At the end of the school year, if the chain reaches all the way around the room, we will have a full-day celebration."

Tommy was excited and couldn't wait to earn a link. During center time, he let Laura go first in a game. He thought to himself, *That was kind, but no one noticed.*

Later in the day, he let a friend go ahead of him in line in music class. Again, no one noticed his kindness, and he began to feel frustrated.

When Tommy got home from school, he felt very upset. *Will I ever get a link?* he wondered.

The next day, Jack, a new student, joined Ms. Tracey's class. He looked a little scared, so without even thinking about it, Tommy walked up to him and said, "Hi, I'm Tommy. Would you like to play with us? You can use my dinosaur!"

Jack smiled and said, "I would love to!"

In the classroom, Ms. Tracey announced,
"Tommy helped Jack feel welcomed.
Let's add our first link to the Kindness Chain!"

KINDNESS
STARTS
HERE

The next day, Jack saw Regina drop her box of supplies. He rushed over to help her pick them up.

"Thank you, Jack!" Regina said, seeming relieved.

Ms. Tracey added a yellow link to the chain.
"I love how you helped Regina pick up her supplies!
That was very kind!" she said.

KINDNESS STARTS HERE

The following day, Regina noticed that Nicole could not zip her coat. "Let me help you," she said.

Regina showed Nicole how to work the zipper, and she pulled it up all by herself.

Another link was added!

Lion

During outside time, the students were on the playground.
When Kristin came back from speech therapy,
the other children were already playing in groups.
She looked unsure and stood by the fence.

Nicole invited her to join her group.

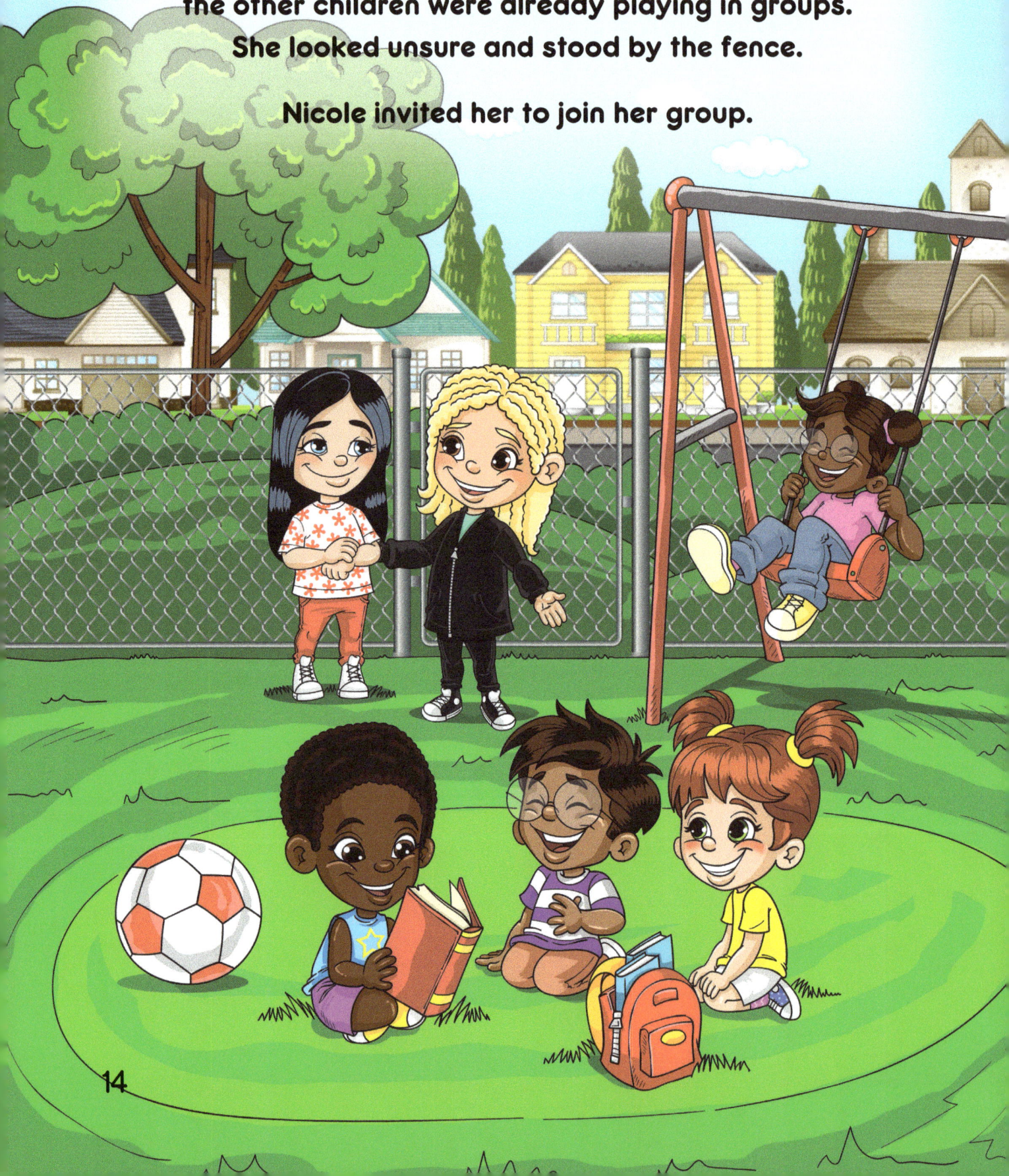

NESS
RTS

John shared his lunch with Lara.

Kristin drew John a lion.

Rose brought everyone cookies.

Tony brought his new puppy to show the class.

Joe carried Rose's backpack for her.

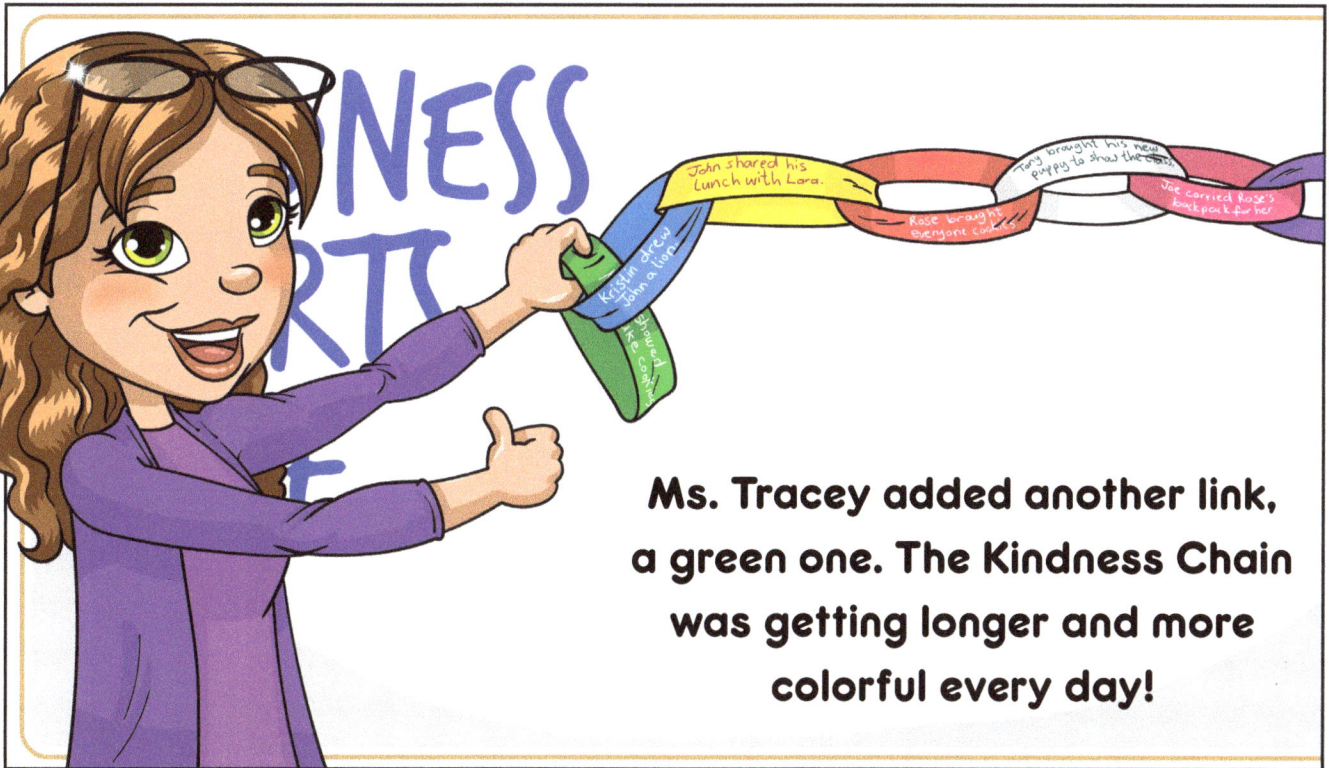

Ms. Tracey added another link, a green one. The Kindness Chain was getting longer and more colorful every day!

Lara gave Joe a big hug!

Jen said thank you to Tony 5 times today.

Jack helped Regina to pick up her supplies.

Tommy let a friend go ahead of him in a line.

Rose held J[...] han[...]

ed Jack welcome.

Regina zipped up Nicole's coat.

Nicole invited Kristin to join her group.

Tony shared his veggies with Jen.

Soon, other students started to perform their own acts of kindness. Tony shared his art supplies.

CLASS

Joe held the door for the class.

John sat with a student who was
alone at the peanut-free table,

and Jen comforted
a younger student
who was sad.

With each kind act, a new link.

The classroom walls were soon covered with a beautiful,

colorful chain that reflected so much kindness.

Jen and Rose cleaned their tables.

Joe picked up Rose's books.

Jen sang happy birthday to Joe.

Lora helped Jack carry his backpack.

Tommy rescued a bee!

Nicole baked Tommy carrot cupcakes.

Ms. Tracey to say thanks.

Joe rescued a bird!

Lora gave her apple to Antonio for lunch.

John helped Rose carry her homework to class.

Jack brought the whole class fresh muffins.

Kristin helped Jack stand up after he fell.

John complimented Joe on his new hair cut.

Jen told Regina how to draw a puppy.

Tommy and Jack brought the class flowers.

Rose held the d for Ms. Frantino

Regina told Lora a nice story about 2 penguins.

Nicole helped Rose finish her cat painting.

When it was almost the end of the school year, Ms. Tracey announced, "Let's take our Kindness Chain down from the wall and stretch it across the front of the school to see how far our kindness has spread this year."

The students carefully held the chain and helped stretch it in front of the school. It reached from one end to the other —a bright, colorful reminder of all their kind deeds.

Principal Frantino and the rest of the school came
to see the chain and praised the students
for their teamwork and kindness all year.

Amazed at how long their Kindness Chain was,
Ms. Tracey's students were so proud of what
they had done!

Ms. Tracey asked, "How can we celebrate all the kindness you have spread?"

The children chose a fun day filled with bubbles and water activities. They played together and shared good times. It was a wonderful day that made their hearts happy!

Tommy looked at the long chain and felt proud.
Kindness can start with one person, one classroom,
one school, one town, one state, one country,
and spread all over the world, he thought. It really
does make the world a better place for us all!

Start your own Kindness Chain and see how far your kindness can spread. Remember that every act of kindness, no matter how small, can make a difference!

With over twenty-five years of experience in publishing and illustration, Jeanine has brought countless characters, stories, and book covers to life—especially in the world of children's books. She began her career designing console games before moving into comics, publishing, and brand design. Her diverse, imaginative style has earned her a Moonbeam Children's Book Gold Award for Best Illustrator. Today, she combines her storytelling expertise with deep industry experience to help clients create captivating books that truly stand out.

Tracey Roegiers is a retired special education preschool teacher who spent more than thirty-five years nurturing young hearts and minds. Tracey's classroom was a place where kindness bloomed, curiosity thrived, and every child felt seen and valued.

Now enjoying retirement, she treasures time with her loving husband, their two wonderful children, their amazing spouses, and two beautiful grandsons. Their family is completed by two cuddly dogs who bring joy to each day.

Inspired by the compassion she witnessed in her students and the unwavering support of her family and friends, Tracey wrote this book to celebrate the everyday acts of kindness that connect us all. She hopes her story encourages children to lead with empathy and reminds readers of all ages that small acts of love and kindness can make a big difference in our world and hearts.

www.ingramcontent.com/pod-product-compliance
Lightning Source LLC
LaVergne TN
LVHW070836080426
835509LV00027B/3487